Lovebook

unto the measure of the stature of the fullness of poetry

*written by Adrian N. Carter,
inspired by Dr. Deryl G. Hunt, Sr., Ph.D.*

Published by
ICB Productions, Inc.
Miami, FL

Published by ICB Productions
P.O. Box 69-3573 Miami FL 33269

Carter Development Group, LLC
www.cartermusiclab.com
cartermusiclab@aol.com
855-265-2328

ISBN: 978-0-9815013-4-5
Published 2013

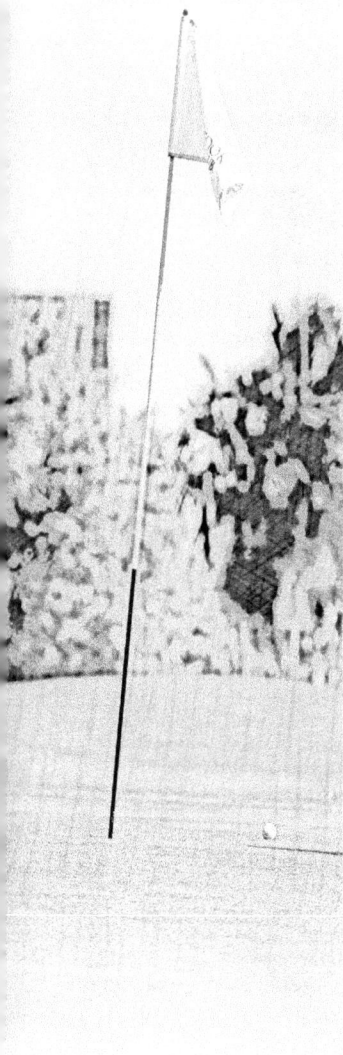

Dedicated to my mentor and friend,
Deryl G. Hunt Sr., Ph.D.

"There's an early worm for the early bird and a late worm for the late bird."

Synopsis of *Lovebook*

Lovebook is a rich collection of poems inspired by the tenants of The Ellison Model, the 7 Step Process (GOMABCD), and biblical teachings that capture the essence of love and spirituality. In parabolic ways it tackles the world system of politics, religion, education, marriage, socialization, and personal issues encountered by individuals on their life journeys.

Recognizing these conflicts in the world system, Lovebook presents a formula to reconcile, restore, and sustain individuals from skewed notions of love that beset them from coming to perfection. Overall, Lovebook is a very positive, encouraging and imploring collection of poems that introspectively looks at love in ways that may not have been evident before. Each poem must be revealed as to the deeper meaning – there is more than what meets the eye. Lovebook contains several poetic formats including cinquains, haikus, free form, sonnets, and universal (an original format created by Adrian N. Carter).

Cinquain (sing-keyn)
A class of poetic forms that employ a 5-line pattern. Earlier used to describe any five-line form, it now refers to one of several forms that are defined by specific rules and guidelines (en.wikipedia.org/wiki/Cinquain). Line one: subject, line two: two words describing the subject, line three: three verbs describing the actions of the subject, line four: four word statement about the subject, and line five: a one-word synonym of the subject.

Haikus (hahy-koo)
A development of the Japanese haiku poetic form in the English language. Common practices in English include: use of three lines, 17 syllables, traditionally in "5-7-5" form, allusion to nature or the seasons, use of a caesura or kire represented by punctuation, space, a line-break, or a grammatical break to compare two images implicitly (en.wikipedia.org/wiki/Haiku_in_English).

Sonnets (son-it)
A Shakespearean, or English, sonnet consists of fourteen lines written in iambic pentameter, a pattern in which an unstressed syllable is followed by a stressed syllable five times. The rhyme scheme in a Shakespearean sonnet is a-b-a-b, c-d-c-d, e-f-e-f, g-g; the last two lines are a rhyming couplet (en.wikipedia.org/wiki/Sonnet).

Universal
The Universal poetic format expands the one directional reading of a poem to multi-dimensional reading, allowing lines or stanzas to sensibly flow no matter the order in which the poem is read. For example, the poem may be read from bottom to top, left to right, right to left, or through random selection of lines or stanzas. The poem has no beginning or end and the more directions in which it can sensibly flow, the more "universal" the poem. The author, Adrian N. Carter, created the Universal poetic format.

Contents

About the Inspiration
Preface
Many Waters Cannot Quench My Love (Haiku)............................ 1
Circle 2
Jehovah's Witness... 4
Jump Ball 5
Haters (Cinquain) 7
Thoughts Unloving 8
I Am Fashion 9
Statue of Love 11
Institutions of Love (Crown Cinquain)...................................... 12
Lost In Me 13
Early Bird, Late Worm (Sonnet) 15
Your Love Is (Haiku Grand Jury) 16
Dedicated to the Memory of... 18
The World, the Flesh, the Devil 19
Desiring to Enter Another Threshold of Heaven 22
Overcomer (Sonnet)... 23
Just Ice 24
Well-done Communities 25
Timed Travel 26
Ending from the Beginning 28
The L-Word 30
Lovemaking (Cinquain) 32
What You Said 33
18th Hole, Pick up Your Ball 34
About the Author 37
Closing Remarks on Love by Elijah Stevens 39

About the Inspiration

Deryl G. Hunt's higher education consisted of a B. A. Degree in Sociology from Fort Valley State College, a M. A. in Sociology from Atlanta University,and a Ph.D. in Public and International Affairs from the University of Pittsburgh. Dr. Hunt has held administrative and faculty appointments at:Miami Dade Community College, University of Pittsburgh, Southern Illinois University, National Office of Housing and Urban Development (GS 15), and the city of Opa-locka, Florida.

In 2000, Dr. Hunt developed The Ellison Model Management Plan. He followed up with the development of a Conflict Resolution model that has been used in training in the US as well as other countries including Panama, Haiti, and the Bahamas. He received the William R. Jones Most Valuable Mentor Award 2000-2001 from the Florida McKnight Foundation for his mentoring model and Florida International University's Multicultural Programs and Services' Inclusive Community Building Founders Award. Dr. Hunt's mentoring model is the subject of four doctoral dissertations and at least three master thesis. Dr. Hunt has also written a dozen dramatic interactive diversity plays with original scores as part of his community building work. Dr. Hunt's extensive training experience ranges locally, nationally, and internationally in working with waste industry line workers and supervisors to military officers, lawyers,government officials and corporate executives.

Preface

I have known Deryl G. Hunt Sr., Ph.D. for the past 25 years as a pastor, author, scholar, professor, consultant, supervisor, event planner, fund-raiser, comic, tennis player, golfer, and visionary. I have watched him for years be outspoken and disciplined in his commitment to reach a higher plateau of spirituality, and to bring those around him up to that plateau. As an undergraduate student at Florida International University, I was privileged to work alongside Dr. Hunt, where he served as Associate Director of the Office of Multicultural Programs and Services, while he developed The Ellison Model. As a Student Government member and later, Student Body President, together, Dr. Hunt and I collaborated in hosting various events, including an annual fundraiser for international students called "The Black Tie Affair."

Dr. Hunt is an avid golfer. I have played winning golf as a part of a four-some with Dr. Hunt, his eldest son, Dexter Hunt, and my father, Dudley Carter since 2010. The experience has been rife with endless life lessons. While we enjoy the game for the fellowship and fresh air, the elements of golf have proven to be an appropriate parallel for overcoming life obstacles as we persevere from hole to (w)hole utilizing skillful play amidst conflict-ridden terrains. Understanding our purpose for playing golf has led to the development of Networking on the Green, a leadership curriculum that incorporates the tenants of The Ellison Model, using the metaphoric nature of golf to teach inclusion, multicultural appreciation, mentorship, conflict resolution, and relationship building.

Lovebook, a collection of poems, is dedicated to Dr. Hunt and captures his demonstrated behaviors as a mentor, teacher, and guide, in addition to his teachings on spirituality and inclusive community building. The book is named Lovebook to reflect the core of his heart: the love of God for God's people till we all come unto the measure of the stature of the fullness of Christ (Ephesians 4:13). As such, Dr. Hunt appears as a silent and veiled author of this book.

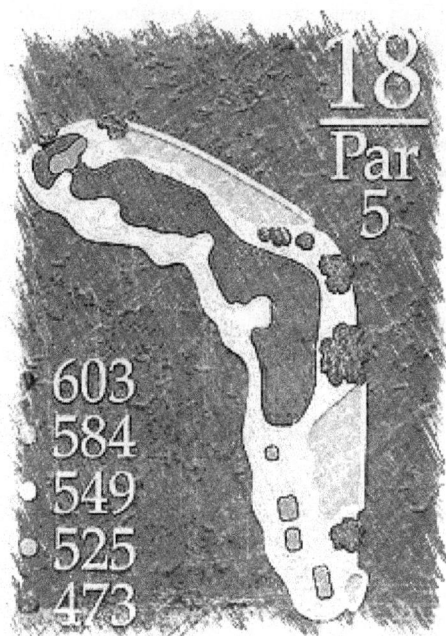

18
Par
5

603
584
549
525
473

Many Waters Cannot Quench My Love, a Haiku

Love is like soft rain,
A tickling baptism –
Eighteen holes of golf.

Circle

"I love the Lord because He first loved me"
is how the song goes.
of course He loved me first;
He knew me before the foundation of the earth
He loved me when time –
well, when there was no such thing.
He loved me before an atom and nucleus
knew to be lovers.
He loved me before love had any other
definition;
when love was defined as love.
I love Him too.
though He loving me first is half the view.

> we rationalize and contextualize,
> in other words humanize,
> in the process humiliate and falsify
> what humans say symbolize love
> but love, all four letters,
> as simple and powerful as God himself,
> can only be actualized as His Christ,
> once crucified in order to purify,
> for God so loved the world that He gave
> His only begotten sun
> to the dark side of the moon and
> while he returned soon, nevertheless
> God loved us so much that He
> sacrificed his love.

I love the Lord because He first loved me,
for loving me was a part of He
that in the creation of me,
was created love returned,
called love and loyalty.
I love Him because the choice
has been made easy to see,
to love Him is to love me.
before the foundation of the earth
He outlined my destiny,
and I quote, "to rest in me"
for to be one with He is to be
the son that He loved first,

loved unselfishly,
for He gave his only begotten son
for all of we to become one
with He and love Him because
He first loved me.

Jehovah's Witness

Heard	about the man
Inquired	of him
Attended	the conference
Met	the people
Reviewed	the material
Traveled	to the Bahamas
Read	the books
Disagreed	with aspects
Observed	the proceedings
Denounced	the teachings
Watched	the man
Sat	in service
Accused	the brethren
Frowned	up your nose
Listened	to the sermon
Misjudged	God's power
Witnessed	the growth
Learned	little by little
Appreciated	over time
Remained	in prayer
Repented	for your attitude
Testified	of the love
Yearned	for more
Studied	the model
Wrote	checks of support
Participated	as a moderator
Resolved	your inner-conflict
Defended	the man
Unified	in humility
Built	inclusive community
Honored	to whom it was due
Trusted	God's ordained
Respected	the message
Cared	about Cordele
Shared	your mistakes
Loved	your stay at Linda's
Modeled	as did Christ
Overcame	the world, the flesh, the devil, and death
Transitioned	to the seventh heaven
Fulfilled	God's word

4

Jump Ball

it's good to know what team you play for
after which, there's no need to say more.
wrestle for righteousness as the law runs loose on the court
hustle for the word that subs in to show support.
get after it, for after it is more.
more for the taking, more to give,
more to understand, more life to live,
and in the process of sweat and twisted ankles,
a lot more to forgive.

Jump ball

jump for the ball,
it's your only option to stay in the game.
It's the only medicine
for the hard court press of pain.
relax,
for you walk in the Spirit and run the game,
jump for the ball, jump in His name.
four quarters cannot establish the pace.
jump ball for your life is the case
that railing accusations are brought before the judge.
but the courtship of love gives you crossover moves
when in cross-examination so defenders can't budge.
for your defense is in the hope, charity,
and obedience of love.

Jump ball

go get it, it's yours.
go after it like bonfires get after s'mores.
like knobs get after doors.

jump high, tip the ball to your teammate.
dribble, pass, tip your hat in courtesy and
share a glass of understanding and peace.
be whole by being a piece of the answer.
shoot without the "ah man" and shucks.

drive to the whole.
mis-shots are not mishaps,
just necessary opportunities to
hustle, rebound, re-attain.

Jump ball

That's love.
jump for your brother's success;
for your sister's progress;
for your child's egress;
for your favorite persons deepness of
honesty, trust, and respect
their journey on the court.
it's never a time to abort.
missions bring missiles and pistols and
gnashing of teeth with gristles and issues.
but jump ball for the winning shot.
you were made in the image and likeness
for this moment.

Jump.

Haters, a Cinquain

Haters
Jealous, ignorant
Gossiping, backstabbing, lying
Always in someone's business
Unwatchful

Thoughts Unloving

You thought...
> the program should have been managed better
> the handouts should have been in color
> the food should have been served earlier
> they should have sung a different song
> the sun was too hot to be outside
> the children were making too much noise
> they should have used a different version of the bible
> they should have collected an offering
> you gave enough in tithes and offerings
> the pastor should have asked you first
> service time was too late in the day
> service was too frequent in the week
> the pastor just let anyone in the church
> you should have been the senior pastor
> so-and-so should have married you-know-who
> her momma ain't raise her in the Lord
> someone should have a word with her
> her shoes didn't match her dress
> her hat wasn't fit for the occasion
> her make-up was too heavy
> his suit color was too loud
> they can't afford to have all those children
> the deacon should have been your husband
> it was too soon for him to die
> you loved.

I Am Fashion

I Am Fashion,
My favorite clothing line
Custom made apparel
To 'dress my state of mind
Tailor's name, Passion
Look back in time
Was always in style
This tailor's design
Conservative and liberal
Both at the same time
A palette of colors
To leave One sublime
Many struggle
To keep up with the trend
Undress themselves
And put on sin
But even then
When faced with problems
Dingy with issues
About to hit bell-bottoms
A jacket of mercy
From a mentoring friend
To warm cold hearts
And 'dress us again
And deliver us from
How we pretend
Shows up in God's timing
To give us a hem.
I Am Fashion,
Dressed to impress
Stitched with a
Breastplate of righteousness
Taught my calling
And appropriateness
For when called to cook
I'm dressed as a chef
When called to travel
I'm dressed as a guest
When called to run
I'm dressed in my sweats
When called home

I'm dressed in my best
Outfit that fits
My God's request
Love is the material
I Am is the brand
Girt about with truth
I know who's *I Am*
Materialistic for heavenly things
And materialized
As the Christ of God that
No photography can surmise.
Logo, shield of faith
Gift card, shop for free
Arrive wearing *I Am* Fashion
States *I Am* sent me
I Am Fashion,
Winter clothing line
Exact set of clothes
For the troubled mind
Fall clothing fits
During sundry times
Colors of encouragement
To back you with a spine
Dried out, overheated
Blind leading the blind
Rest can be found in the
Summer collection line
Springtime couture
Reminds us all is fine
Future bright pastels
Observing miracles and signs
This is high fashion
On the high runway of life
A living mannequin
Of the man *I Am* in Christ
All else is a fad
Their jewelry line is fake
In my person *I Am* made over
All else impersonates
Eleason's menswear of preparation
Ellen's hats of salvation
I Am Fashion,
Dressed for every occasion.

10

Statue of Love

only love can make love fall in love,
then fall in love again,
the most beautiful incurable cure is love,
in which Violet fell.
while the outside showed someone stricken in age,
growing, bearing no leaves
who can find a virtuous woman
in whom God can say I am well pleased?
this is one great mystery.

it appears to eat away the senses,
take away the tongue,
take the strength to fight,
take the desire to run.
dormant. still. un-moved. unknowing.
slender, unseeming.
un-growing, needing.
only left to one state of mind,
called constantly believing.
the place where God has called us all to be.
fasting from this world,
in need of God's constant care.
constantly relying on the tenderness He shares.

and as God made man and woman
in His image and likeness,
and told Arnold tend to the garden,
at all cost, no matter what the price is.
it was all for the purpose, beginning and end,
that love could fall in love all over again.
reaching new depths in Christ
in whom we can only depend.
and again, let love fall deeper in love
and fall deeper again.
uncovering a greater love of God
to make us all repent.
this is the great mystery revealed
of the statue God erected,
so you and I can look on and know
what it is to be perfected.

Tribute to
Violet Bernice Williams

11

Institutions of Love, a Crown Cinquain

Love
Kind, long-suffering
Was, is, will
Sent manna from heaven
Savior

Love
Accessible, responsible
Collaborating, legislating, participating
Eradicate hunger and poverty
Manifesto

Love
Year-round, precocious
Involving, instructing, instilling
No child left behind
Legacy

Love
Professional, priceless
Buying, selling, distributing
Housing market bubble burst
Investment

Love
Powerful, reflective
Courting, proposing, submitting
Perfectly joined together as
One

Lost in Me

get thee behind me
you're blocking my view
let's keep it simple
I don't see hue.
what I see just walked in the door
humble as Ozzie's pie
wearing all white
as wonderful as a Fourth of July
fireworks in my heart had never been lit before
and unlike before
I can hear the matches struck
and words whispered
"are you ready to explore?"
"To further more, get lost in me,"
said the voice, "and then get lost some more.
lost like a river out to sea.
lost like birds that fly south and
get caught on the homeliness
of an old lady's balcony.
forget where you came from.
forget what you know.
I am wondrously made and in that wonder
you will grow,
if you get lost in me.
lost like making a new discovery.
make the right turn,
make it in my arms is the rightness to yearn.
Christopher Columbus tried but eventually died.
lost in me means you survive.
don't worry about your outfit or shoes.
you don't need it wear you're going.
they won't fit you for too long at the
rate you'll be growing.
get lost in my eyes,
attached to my smell,
comfortable in the *Circles* I dwell."
the final words
left me subdued
the voice spoke: "let's keep it simple,
I see you."

Early Bird, Late Worm, *a Sonnet*

Early bird rise to obtain daily meal
Early bird with haste, first served to first come
Early worm rise and shine bright with appeal
Early worm moisture on early bird thumb

Late worm, witty, plans for late looking on
Late worm, lethargic, brims at its escape
Late bird, eschewed, too slow at crack of dawn
Late bird, hopeful, moves not at faster rate

Not all birds fly the speed of swift to hear
Purpose must fulfill despite stage of day
That all birds come to overcoming tier
Late worm knows not, a late bird on its way

Adage, only early bird catches worm,
Late worm for late bird, inclusive the term.

Your Love Is, a Haiku Grand Jury

your love is better
than the praise of achievement
from thousands of men.

your love is better
than what natural minds may
try to comprehend.

your love is better
than aspiring to make
something of myself.

your love is better
than combined social networks
vast amass of wealth.

your love is better,
every fantasy come
true does not compare.

your love is better,
everything else I have
tried does not come near.

your love is sweeter
than a kiss on the cheek from
grandmothers who care.

your love is sweeter
than the sound of victory
erupting with cheers.

your love is sweeter,
caramelized sugar has
not the slightest chance.

your love is sweeter,
giving homemade lemonade
not the slightest glance.

your love is warmer
than a Miami vacay
with money to spend.

your love is warmer
than birthday celebrations
with age old best friends.

your love is truer
than the protection we give
from burglars who snoop.

your love is truer
than the best intentions of
neighborhood watch groups.

your love is stronger
than the resolve women have
when pushing life out.

your love is stronger
than the will to move forward
when bordered by doubt.

your love is, verdict
read, better than all that has
been implied and said.

Dedicated to the memory of...

The Lord giveth and taketh away
Never can we judge but always pray
That the passing of a friend helps to pave a brighter way
So the future of the present brings about a better day
Minus the physical added to the spiritual
Michael the Archangel, fly in the spiritual
Wings spread apart to the clouds so high
I can still see the smile and the twinkle in his eye

I can still hear his laugh ringing through his mouth
Kindhearted sums up what Mike was all about
So I'm more than content that his time was well-spent
Impacting lives – a very huge dent
Remain confident so when the time comes
We walk with him satisfied with what we've done
Given over to the Spirit that leads to success
Knowing with God's strength we did our very best

They say it's inevitable and can't be cheated
But we know otherwise, it must be defeated
Cause the struggle of life can leave one depleted
The power to overcome is what is needed
For every Mike minused and Burroughs buried
That brings sadness to the heart and leaves some worried
Know joy always comes in the morning time
The same way the sun is always guaranteed to shine

Shed tears, have dreams, and question why
Read scriptures, meditate, and pray to the most high
But after the fact and after the pain
The silver lining is that there's always something more to gain
So I remain: hopeful, determined, and committed to the cause
For I will never view their passing as a loss
They're in a better place, walking in His grace
I can only thank them for building up my faith

Sankofa

Tribute to Tim Burroughs and Mike Minus

The World, the Flesh, and the Devil

I've been looking for my mother to love me
but how could she know?
she was brought up in an era of servitude,
taught to be responsible
for her younger siblings at the age of two
she wasn't taught to love –
she was taught to run errands and don't make errors
she was 16 and pregnant
grandma told her "I love you"
but words without support
are playgrounds for the imagination to create feelings of being hurt
"Knock, knock."
"Who is it?"
"I need you to run to the store and get some bouillon and ice. I love you."
"Okay mom. I love you too."
and it's back to reality, back to work.
so mom didn't teach me love,
she taught me something else.
she taught survival,
get enough pennies to purchase b's and y's and just get by.
she taught defense
be on the defense, ready to fight,
even when you're wrong.
she taught to just do me
put myself first, even if I have to serve others
(an inconvenience to doing me).
mom liked to say, "I love you my baby."
but grandma never taught mom how to love
mom doesn't know how.

I've been looking for myself to love me
but how could I know?
I was birthed in sin and iniquity
in need of divinity,
membership to angels alcohol anonymous
in need of recovery,
oh, how my soul sought vanity.
so I bought large mirrors with make-up kits
to make up shit,
I shadowed the outline of my minds image of success,
I gave mouth service with black crabbing colors

glossed on my lips,
and when I ran out of ideas
I bought more make it up kits,
I didn't know love.
I loved myself, but not really.
I loved the feeling I got of
thinking I loved myself.
but the love I had brought me closer to hell.
lust and greed,
and the more I found a need
for only what I wanted
is the more I found a heart un-yielded and haunted,
but I called it love.
I loved the sound of my name,
I loved the accolades of my claims,
I loved the sense of my gain,
I loved my story from rags to fame.
this was vain running through my veins
oh wretched man I was
this can't be, won't ever be love.

I've been looking for my wife to love me
but how could she know?
she don't respect no man
she's still trying to understand
why daddy always had other plans
she don't know how to love me
how can she when the first man in her life
never loved her right
when she's been sad all her life
fought by thoughts that quietly bite
daddy made promises he couldn't keep
not even a farm with sheep to count for sleep
so daddy's little daughter grew up weak
and each week when pastor preached
he seemed more steeped in making headroom
for daddy to keep being bleak
honor thy mother and thy father was the decree

"but why daddy don't seem to have no time for me?"
"daddy never played house with me."
"daddy never went to the movies with me."

"daddy never said he'd do anything for me."
so how could she love
when all other men are progenies
biological reflections
of what had hurt her most in society
but daddy never taught daughter how to love
wife doesn't know how.

Desiring to
Enter
Another
Threshold of
Heaven

To align, first flatline
Our thoughts, our deeds, our wires
Devices for which we pay prices
That prevents us from growing higher
We know the Enemy is a liar
Yet somehow seems to get what he requires
To fan flames of disdain to ignite fires
Glamoured by vampires, guilty with priors
Sit, wait, and conspire
Against love without price that waits for a buyer
For Alfonso's sake
Know the situation is dire
Change up your desire
So your interview with Christ
Can make you a lovely hirer
Desire to Enter Another Threshold of Heaven
Dead to the flesh and desires that leaven
Sharper than a two-edged sword
Let love cut the umbilical cord
And birth you once more
As a clergyman, a legislator, an educator,
An investor, a spouse, a mentor
Who lives and loves from the core.

Death to using the N-word out of disrespect
Death to pride, inebriation, and cigarettes
Death to forsaking love and marriage and choosing sex

Death to the world system when governed by greed
Death to overlooking the poor with obvious needs
Death to giving offerings in church to cover up misdeeds

Death to the addictions that are killing dreams
Death to the love of money and the problems it schemes
Death to the lust of the flesh, high heels, and form-fitting jeans

And live.

Overcomer, a Sonnet

Merciful and tender are your blessings
Providing means to meet at every end
Whom you love we know that they are chasen
To raise us up to walk with you as friends

Journeys beyond the dusts of mans' design
Transcending earth to overcome and reign
Perfecting in a Godly state of mind
Maturing as I learn to love again

For I have learned no other thought than love
To know that you and I are made to last
Your greatest gift that came from up above
To open gates with life of bliss so vast

I am reflecting everything that's right
The power and wisdom of God's own Christ.

Just Ice

Justice is cold, just ice
Gotta keep a cool walk, the fridge type
So if the cops yell freeze any given night
You can stay still and chill like a water pipe

Situation ain't about wrong or right
Or if your skin's dark or your eye's light
It's spiritual warfare not a natural fight
Meant to cause division, don't believe the hype

Brothers please get ya pray on
Peter's locked up but an angel got his Freon
Troy Davis was bought with a price
Though they pushed him out of water into just ice

Take heed that your cup isn't filling up
Demons are television, they be acting up
Give thanks to God, He gotta plan
Third level of faith, there's hope for man.

Tribute to Troy Davis

Well-done Communities

Well-done communities seasoned with honesty,
Taste sweet to me, nice aroma,
Tilt your head back, put your nose in the air,
Get a whiff, hmmm, smells like Goma.
Tenderly prepared, you can see the time and care,
Went into making sure it's proportionately shared.
Give me a mouthful or bite size,
It's easy going down and warm on the inside.
It's delicious, and certainly nutritious,
Even the waiting time is more than judicious.
Ingredients the richest, quality's the highest,
Streets are the cleanest, lights are the brightest.
We're each a community, building community,
Delicately prepared by hands of unity.
Keep building 'till the day comes
Goma puts an arm around you and says well-done.

*Originally written for the Cordele Youth Summer Institute program,
a character development program for middle and high school students hosted in
Cordele, Georgia.*

Timed Travel

Carry me,

Off to a distant place that's close to me
Surround me with your grace, upholding me
Let me look upon your face, beholding me
In such a glorious space, abode in me
Giving up all my ways, unfolding me
Where abides faith, hope, and charity

New stars beyond moons we see
Unchartered waters where waters seem not be
Beautiful galaxy

Carry me,

Tribute to Helen Ellison, Ed.D.,
former Associate Vice-Presi-
dent, Student Affairs at Florida
International University, for
whom The Ellison Model was
named in honor of her dem-
onstrated skillful approach
to establishing a harmonious
environment of diverse indi-
viduals in the work place and
her caring, sharing, and loving
attitude.

To a place that's kin to me
Where my brothers and sisters wait for me
Apparently, jokingly, wistfully
Enjoying each moment of the ride
Parade through the sky as planets go by
Waving high
They line up to glimpse the passerby

Dedicated to present me spotless before Christ
Without wrinkle or blemish in my life

Arrive upon a thousand horses
Chariots of knights and light
Walk no more upon sandy shores
But upon everything made right
For out of these the greatest is love
And you loved me 'till love turned me right
Into the image and like, of His nest
Perfected and matured into perfect rest

How peaceful the journey,
How scenic the view,
How honored I am to be loved by you
If only they knew, dreams come true
Far exceeding all I knew
More breathtaking than morning's dew

Carry me,

To where words are few
And the quickness to hear
Reflects the model of angels who share
And care, and love, and fear
In reverence of community building engineers

Ingenuity of genuine love
Erecting edifices of grace
A shared vision of continuity
To provide God's creatures a place
To uphold, behold, abode and unfold
The sonship of God,
submitted spirit, body, and soul.

Ending from the Beginning, a Universal Quad*

I have finally accepted

In me is perfected

Leaving all notions rejected

The Christ of God projected

Nothing to be percepted

No longer subjected

That I am is reflected

Wherein all has been corrected

To know I am protected	Cannot be neglected
For I have been selected	Loved, honored, and respected
Of me it's expected	Remaining unaffected
Many mansions be erected	Overcoming as directed

The L-Word

Last night I left my wife
Walked in and said it was over
Said I'm starting a new life
Then thru my bag over my shoulder

I closed the door behind me
Leaving all bygones behind
Took no pictures to remind me
No favorite songs to rewind

Got in my car and headed north
Different from my usual route
The wind helped my mind to sort
(Was always cluttered going south)

I don't miss her anymore
And all the bickering we did
No need to try and settle the score
That's not how loving lives

Upon arrival to my new estate
My wife met me at the door
She said she too had to escape
Couldn't live like that anymore

When I first told her I was leaving
She insisted coming along
Despite all prior proceedings
By my side is where she belonged

She left out empty handed
Said all she needed was in my bag
Hated the thought of being left stranded
Confessed I was all she had

Fingers, palms in clasp
Our home, we walked in together
Knowing all that was is past
Onward to peaceful endeavors

Thanked the real-estate agent
Perfect home to start anew
Fully furnished, nothing vacant
Plus a water's edge view

Dinner was exquisite
Catered by Your Savory Fare
Neighbors love to visit
As much as we love to share

Like strings to a symphony
Written by a master composer
We play long days in harmony
As our love grows stronger and older

Two pairs seeing as one
Aligned a single vision
Trilling the sound of overcome
Breathing life into would win decisions

Free as the day created
When wearing clothes had no season
Renaming the once ill fated
Our home, this Garden of Eden.

Lovemaking, a Cinquain

Lovemaking
Playful, edible
Riding, pulling, biting
Sleeping on your chest
Newborn

What You Said

no time no space no reason or rhyme
could keep your words from being
what you said it would be.
when trenches were dug beneath the earth
in attempts to create new foundations,
your roots were cemented in me.
when liars spoke of a destitute land,
I always found nourishment in you.
when boats sailed the oceans
and ships crossed the seas to find new,
you were always closer to me.
closer than close,
we were one single item
on a clothing rack on clearance
in no other color or size.
just one perfect fit for the perfect fit.
covering me from head to feet.
I never knew weakness,
I never knew loss,
I only knew of an absolutionist position
of what you said we were,
of who you said I am,
to where you said I belonged,
to whom.
no talk of the future,
of spaceships and space, no frontiers or
new creatures from a newer place.
no never before seen,
no never before heard,
of hieroglyphics or birds,
no time or space no new sensations of taste.
only what you said mattered.
only what you say is matter.
taking shape to your shape,
solace in your solitude of deepness of voice,
softness of tone, highness of pitch
speedily like I was your own.
yours to own from when you said it
'till now nothing has changed.
meant to be together, nothing can keep us apart.
no time, no space, no reason or rhyme
when you've already said
I am yours and you are mine.

18th Hole, Pick up Your Ball

On the front nine I resolved my conflict,
Freed from the grasp of death,
Going forward with my mission
With every living breath.
No turning back, no digressing
I'm at peace with where I stand,
For obedience and to hearken
Both best the fat of ram.
Know not when my time is come,
But know my time draws near,
Picture perfect in all white
Devoid of any tear.
Wicked is the enemy,
Deceitful in his ways,
By grace, I am submitted,
From the charge I have not swayed.
For no matter what is presented,
Adorned in linen and gold,
I shall only fear the one
Who can destroy body and soul.
Grateful I am called,
Upon a shelf is not my claim,
I did my duty, played the course,
'Till declared I overcame.
I have traveled to all regions,
Planting flags throughout the globe,
Declaring territories,
Causing great swell unto the fold.
Visiting kings upon the throne,
Presidents at the helm,
Leaders of communities,
The dignitaries among men,
The vagabond and proud,
The educated and poor,
And whenever it was necessary,
Drove a little more.
Each trip, a gift,
A souvenir of sort,
To help with your defense of
Trials in every court.
My will, written,

Has been given you by the Son,
I love you my children,
But my work here is done.
Soon the day is come when
The Hosts on high shall call,
And on the 18th hole says,
"Servant, pick up your ball."

About the Author

Born in Trelawny, Jamaica, Adrian migrated to the United States of America at age seven to live with his father and loving stepmother in South Florida. Poetry found him in the third grade as a way to communicate his feelings when frustrated. He penned his first poem entitled "Teachers, teachers are the meanest creatures." Noted for his creative writing skills, by fifth grade Adrian tested into the Gifted Magnet Program for Miami-Dade Public Schools. As Adrian matriculated to middle-school, he competed in the Dade County Youth Fair Poetry Expo, published a poem, and competed in the Miami Dade College Theodore Gibson Oratorical Project, in which he placed third in the finals for two consecutive years in the categories of original work and dramatic monologue.

Adrian's writing has expanded over the years to include short stories and scholastically driven work such as academic essays, journalism articles, and research papers. Ultimately, Adrian is a renaissance individual. In addition to poetry, Adrian is a songwriter, sound engineer, spoken-word artist, music artist, higher education administrator, adjunct educator, co-pastor, and motivational speaker with a strong focus on conflict resolution and leadership development. He also shares a passion for working with the youth in his church and local communities.

Adrian has a bachelor's degree in Mass Communication from Florida International University and a master's degree in Educational Leadership from Florida Atlantic University. He currently resides in Broward County with his loving wife and three children.

*Universal Poetic Format**

Ending From the Beginning uses a poetic format created and dubbed by the author, Adrian N. Carter, as the Universal Poetic Format.

Special Thanks

Special thanks to my dad and mom, Dudley and Joann, for always supporting my passion for writing and music; my wife for being a wonderful mother and source of inspiration; my friend since the fourth grade, Clive, for a childhood filled with memories and enough life-lessons a.k.a. beatings; my place of worship, The Church of Christ Apostolic Nondenominational; my family and friends in the Bahamas; the 7 Steps neo-gospel group; and the 4th Member hip-hop group. Special thank you to the editors and the contributions from Dawn Burgher, John Harvey Jr., Dawn Hunt, Deryl Hunt Jr., Elijah Stevens, and Eleason Williams; pictures provided by Phrame by Phrame Photography. And thank you to my silently boisterous co-author, Deryl G. Hunt, Sr., Ph.D.

Closing Remarks on Love

Never have I before felt
Such an urge to serve and please,
You.
I want to know you,
Speak as you speak,
Love as you love.
My admiration for such beauty is
Overwhelming.
I feel your deep loving concern, and
It is warm.
It compels me to operate
Under your divine nature,
Which is to perfectly yield.
As the waves and tides respond to the
Gravitational pull of the moon,
And sway back and forth,
And as the day and night
Play tag at your word,
I yield wholeheartedly.
My love, sweet love,
You give me reason to
Desire to be with you for eternity,
Our oneness is infinite in glory, and
Our passion is passionate of this love.
Nothing can separate our love,
Burning intensities,
Tantamount to 3000 suns
Isn't too unbearable, for your love
Your love creates such vivid imagery
Of a communication that is able to
Vastly express itself
More capable than anyone can
In their native tongue.
Day unto day the earth
And the fullness thereof
Groans for your love.
Your love is better than,
And the list goes on, but
I would have never known
Unless your love came and
Revealed this unto me.

Lovebook Album

[WDGH, LOVE 108 Radio Show]
Hosted by Crystal "CJ" Harvey and John "JJ" Harvey

[Many Waters Cannot Quench My Love] Performed by Lawrence Darville and David Ritchey. Vocals and guitar by Lawrence Darville.
[Circle] Performed by Nicole Brown.
[Jehovah's Witness] Performed by Eneka Ferguson.
[Jump Ball] Performed by Adrian N. Carter.
[I Am Fashion] Performed Eleason Williams, Adrian N. Carter, Lawrence Darville, and Daphney Carter.
[Institutions of Love] Perfomed by Alvin "A-Stone" Jackson.
[Lost In Me] Performed by Shalicia Frazier.
[Early Bird, Late Worm] Performed by Messiah Barnes.
[Your Love Is] Performed by Patrick Brown, Nicole Brown, Shalicia Frazier, Lawrence Darville, Gwen Evans, Eneka Ferguson, Daphney and Adrian N. Carter, Messiah Barnes and Crystal Barnes. Music performed by Nicole Brown (vocals) and Lawrence Darville (guitar).
[The World, the Flesh, the Devil] Performed by Fran Frazier and Adrian N. Carter.
[Desiring to Enter Another Threshold of Heaven] Performed by Lawrence Darville.
[Overcomer] Performed by Nicole Brown and Patrick Brown.
[Just Ice] Performed by Lawrence Darville.
[Well-done Communities] Performed by Franchesca Yearby.
[Timed Travel] Performed by Gwen Evans.
[The L-Word] Performed by Daphney Carter and Adrian N. Carter. Saxophone by Stanford Thomas.
[What You Said] Performed by John Roundtree.
[Closing Remarks] on Love Performed by Crystal Harvey.

Crystal Harvey, John Harvey, Patrick Brown, Nicole Brown, Shalicia Frazier, Lawrence Darville, Gwen Evans, John Roundtree, Eneka Ferguson, Daphney Carter and Adrian N. Carter appear courtesy of **7 Steps Music**. All music produced, recorded, mixed and mastered by Adrian N. Carter for **The [Carter Music] Lab**.

www.ingramcontent.com/pod-product-compliance
Lightning Source LLC
Chambersburg PA
CBHW061756040426
42447CB00011B/2330